So You Wanna be Italian?

An Artist's Journey Exploring Her Roots

by

Anna Filameno

in collaboration with Christopher Kaufman (editor/artist)

©---Publications 2014

"Anna is a word painter with a vast palette... sometimes romantic and poetic, sometimes explosive! Reading her vignettes is like being on a roller coaster ride... and when you catch your breath you're ready for more!"
                                        -Arlene Karian, Author

"I couldn't put this book down, I wish it never ended!... I am so grateful for this book, Anna's writing brings to light the immense contribution of these... almost mythical figures... the Italian writers, actors, directors, politicians and teachers who have forever enriched our world!"

                            - Diana Nadas, Italian translator and interpreter

"Anna's work is raw and alive, full of ethnic color and flavor. I can think of no better way to spend a few hours, wrapped in her vignettes, lost inside people significant to all of our cultures!"
                            - Ilene Aliyah Alexander, psychotherapist

"Being Italian is an amazing adventure in itself and Anna Filameno has brought us the experience and made it alive for us. It's amazing how I felt my own roots as I read these pages. The graphic art is amazing!"
                            - Alice Cotton Royer, Author, Educator, Artist

"To my cousins Faye, Ada, Jenny, Jeane, Betty and Frances... Those Southern Italian women who taught me to laugh... and to all the adventurers, explorers... free spirits... to all those who look to their roots to explore themselves... in other words... to all my readers..."

Copyright © 2014 by Christopher Kaufman
All rights reserved. This book or any portion thereof may not be reproduced or used in any manner whatsoever without the express written permission of the publisher except for the use of brief quotations in a book review.

Printed in the United States of America First Printing, 2014 ISBN 978-0985960759 / Ingram Spark

Three Dashes Publications
7101 Colonial Road L3C
Brooklyn, New York 11209
soundartus@gmail.com

TABLE OF CONTENTS

STORYTELLERS

Federico Fellini	7
Diane di Prima	13
Luigi Pirandello	18

DREAMERS

Francis Ford Coppola	26
Anna Magnani	31
Roberto Rossellini	36
Eleanora Duse	42

LOVERS

Rudolf Valentino	54
Marta Abba	60
Giacomo Casanova	64

HEROES AND HEROINES

Nicola Sacco & Bartolomeo Vanzetti	71
Tina Modotti	76
Vito Marcantonio	81
Oriana Fallaci	85

OUTCASTS

Maria Licciardi	93
Aradia	98

REBELS

Frank Sinatra	103
Maria Montessori	108
Carlo Tresca	113

A note from Anna

When I was a little girl growing up in the South Bronx the world was filled with... ***a kind of wild openness.*** It appeared that everyone around me was going in different directions... There was a restlessness in the streets that never left me and I was never quite certain of where I belonged.

As I grew up and began my career as an actress and writer, I knew the streets had given me so much to write about, so many ways to tap into the human condition... stuff that as an actress I could draw upon, and yet...

I felt lost...

"Who am I?"... I thought... "And how do I find the pieces of myself that I have lost along the way?"

"And where do I begin?..."

I remember when I was a teenager... I passed a movie theater and found myself staring at a large poster of FEDERICO FELLINI. I stared at that name for a few moments. He was part of the Italian thing... I thought,

"Maybe I should find out what this is all about..."

I entered the theater and as I sat in the darkness, a new world opened up to me... **one of passion and magic...**

I wanted to become a part of it...

"Is this what it means to be Italian?"... Well, it was a good place to start!

So, what did it mean to me... being Italian?

I think of the scene when Sofia Loren is standing half naked in the water of the fountain at Piazza Navona in Rome... of the distinct aroma of steaming garlic and olive oil rising from the freshly made pizza Napoletana being served straight out of the oven... of annual fashion week in Milan, where designers display their genius...

I think of... sitting around the dinner table and everyone's talking at the same time... loudly!... Of when those Sunday dinners became an event rather than a quiet afternoon... and somebody broke out into song... of when I get a chill listening to Frank Sinatra... and Andrea Boccelli...

The contributions of Italians are so wildly diverse... from Dante, Michelangelo, Vivaldi... to the fighter for human rights Vito Marcantonio, the courage of Sacco and Vanzetti... the dark side of La Cosa Nostra and the underbelly of the Roman Empire with all of its indulgences... and I suddenly realized...

The little girl from the South Bronx is one of them!

So if you really want the experience of being an Italian or German or Irish or African American person... If you want to find out who you really are... then maybe you should meet a few of the people who carry the same spirit as do you...

That's what I have done

I discovered who I was by writing these little vignettes...

These are not biographies... rather, they are the collective spirit of Italians all over the world... Perhaps, after reading some of these vignettes, you will recognize that there is...

A little bit of Italian in all of us...

CIAO

— ANNA FILAMENO

STORY TELLERS

I know what I have given you; I do not know what you have received.

-      Antonio Porchia

I begin with the storytellers and dreamers...

the ones that opened me up to a world of microcosms.

They are the ones that broke the chains of convention...

brought transcendence and tore away at the very heart of my soul.

They are the ones that brought freedom to my imagination...

and with them came the spirit of my culture... mysteries of the psyche... the world of drama, prose, poetry... and brought...

Creative magic to a little girl from the South Bronx.

Federico Fellini

"Iconic Dreamer"

"There is no end. There is no beginning. There is only the passion of life."

Sun in Capricorn

Director

FEDERICO,

Last night I had a dream

I was standing in front of molten rock... the hot liquid poured in a steady stream... as it spilled it began taking other forms. Slowly... it slipped away... in its place was an immense black hole with infinite expanse... and yet, I was not afraid.

I felt transformed... I became anchored to something new and impossible that was about to happen. In my dream, I felt I had to make myself available to the change that was taking place... and the very process of waiting was part of the summons.

Yes. I was being summoned

One can pass imperceptibly from one moment to the other and not recognize what is real, that life is moving all around you... that there myriads of fragments constantly changing inside your mind.

Suddenly I was standing in a playground... and I thought...

"Maybe life is meant to be played..."

There were swings and sliding boards and merry-go-rounds. Clowns began dancing around the monkey bars and making somersaults. There was music... and winds came with enormous bubbles, all colorful and bright.

There was the sensation of movement... and I felt a kind of rhythm inside I had never felt before... as though I were newly inventing myself. Things were growing and changing and I grew strong and voluptuous and wicked. *The world around me was colossal....*

I saw dimensions I had never noticed before... layers of intricate woven forms... and I was faced with a perception as though it was all about to swallow me up...

It was as though I could be whatever I dared to be

Could this be freedom, I wondered? Was I so free to fly in my own orbit that I didn't fit into anything except my own story? Could I do things that were not expected of me?

I saw it... My story... My own truth... and as I stared into my own truth...

It scared the hell out of me...

I sat up and suddenly realized I was not dreaming. I was in a Fellini movie!

Fellini. Transformer. Dreamer. Visionary. Seducer. A man in search of himself. Wild man. Liar.

What is the meaning of your films he was often asked?

"I don't understand them either," he answered. *"I don't seem capable of even suggesting an interpretation."*

Who was the man who gave language another meaning? Who never betrayed his unconscious or his intuition?

That is the reason you were a liar, Federico... because truth is subjective and is only a story we tell ourselves. Truth is the last fabrication. It is the last expression at the end of a journey. It is subject to change, illusion, judgments ...*excuses.* Truth covers our nakedness. Truth is exaggerated.

Tell us your lies, Federico!

Tell us we are allowed to live in our fantasies, in our lies... tell us we are allowed to explore... to believe in the imagination and to have the freedom to evolve.

The imagination is a kaleidoscope

Your films are free spaces where you let yourself dream... where anything is possible. That is your legacy and the great gift you have given the world. The excitement is not in the communication or in the essence of the message but in the anticipation ...*the waiting for it.* The message becomes ecstasy and the biggest tragedy is when we give up the dream because our dreams are the only things that give us passion to live.

Federico, Dreams have their own soul

A vortex of images and sensations rise within me like a sea of invention. Visions and color and wild, wild places... women with huge breasts, the magic realm between the exaggerated softness... a place of delirium... People flying... faces and masks, a world of symbols, desire and passion... A universe of surrealistic memories, the fragmented psyche, the restless libido... the evolution of the unconscious to all those mad, mad places.

You got a problem with that?

Diane di Prima
"Fire Storm"

"The only war is the war against the imagination."

Sun in Leo

Beat poet

Poet laureate of San Francisco

Her Own Road

Sometimes a road takes you to a place that you had not intended...

It's not a path anyone else has taken and it has no end. Not anyone can travel on that road because it is your road and all the twists and turns will take you to a place you've never been before... because imagination is the road sign you follow.

Why do we choose one road that precludes all the others? Why take that one? The one curving with twists and turns... and which runs past rambling forests and open spaces and never leads in a straight line?

That first step...

Where will it take you? The road is long and winding and it has no boundaries and in the distance the sun is reflecting on the road ahead. Are we to wander through our dreams? How long? Roads always take us somewhere. Do we know where we are going?

And what about the woman who creates her own path?

DIANE DI PRIMA, you were an important writer of the beat movement... you loved Zen and Buddhism and Sanskrit... and Alchemy... and raised five children...

So many roads, Diane

Who stands in the sun? Who was meant for these...

Firestorms?

There was a whole generation of women racing through a decade of rebellion and you carried the flame. Loba, the she-wolf. Woman's consciousness set ablaze in a stream of poetry. Wolf symbolism.

DIANE, you wrote:

"I have come to know myself
And have gathered myself from everywhere..."

From everywhere. From the beginning. Lilith. Mary Magdalene. The ancient whores who gave their bodies to impulse, their sensualities to nature and have dared to live with solitude.

The Loba goddess, the one you wrote about, Diane... the unearthing of the female connecting us to our strength and dreams... So much of you, Diane, has gone into the uncovering.

What do we find when we look there?

Dynamic life force. The firestorm.

Where is the Loba goddess now?

She has been a powerful light, tenacious and wild... emerging between the stones and mountains... bubbling hot springs ignite her fire as she provokes the world with her poems. The earth demands conquest, yet it is warm like the womb... and the litany of her song carries the weight of centuries... of the women who have lived before us... who have broken through the crust of the earth demanding their place in the sun.

Firestorms

DIANE, is that what freedom is all about?... You were the woman who danced to a different drum... ...*the source* ... and we were all there together in our jeans and running shoes... with our flags and banners and our secrets... we separated from our mothers because we had to, and defined our sisters because we needed to.

The women of the 60's.

We were there with our legacy

We stood with you because you were one of the great writers and we were impatient and we wanted the continuity of our voices... *immediately*... and we are still riding the wave of sisterhood.

How far are you from those days in Brooklyn?... When you stood in the shadow of your grandfather... an associate of Carlo Tresca and Emma Goldman? A young girl armed only with her poetry, deciding which road to take?

A road is as long as you make it

And Diane, where would you have gone if you had not taken that one?

Luigi Pirandello

"finding the author"

Sun in cancer

Nobel Prize in Literature

"I have tried to tell something to other men, without any ambition,

except perhaps that of avenging myself for having been born."

LUIGI,

Characters have a way of finding their way into the mind of an author. They become adamant and want to be found, discovered... explained and above all, to sound their own voice. They seek the right author. They seek a master who can give them the life they deserve... one that will set them free to express their truth, whatever that might be.

Characters maintain many levels of awareness. They are always in revolt against preconceived notions as to who they are. They want to be spontaneous and wild and untamed and do whatever the hell they want to. They definitely do not want to be kept silent.

And just look who they found!

Pirandello

They found you, **LUIGI PIRANDELLO**,... you, who gave your characters an audience, presented them the venue to speak, argue, confront, love and who conceded that they had a mind of their own.

Your characters were all in revolt and played against the mask of reality and the emptiness of illusion.

You said,

"Whatever is a reality today, whatever you touch and believe in and that seems real for you today, is going to be - like the reality of yesterday - an illusion tomorrow."

There were plays, novels, short stories... and your characters continued to crowd you... They arrived in enormous volume... with their insanity, craziness, death, bitterness, disillusionment, unpredictability and paradoxes. They invaded your brilliance... you, who gave them permission to enter the playground of your mind and share the reflections of your personal experience.

We know so little of the author until we probe his dependency on his characters and the obsession with them, the ones that come to him from the labyrinth of his soul. The characters have found him. They belong to him. He gives them life and once given their freedom, they are on their own.

"Whoever has the luck to be born a character can laugh even at death. Because a character will never die! A man will die, a writer, the instrument of creation: but what he has created will never die!"

You were true to your first wife and held fast to your marriage to a woman who suffered a mental breakdown... But at the moment you first laid eyes on Marta Alba, you knew by instinct and some mysterious intuition that you had found *...your muse.*

Marta

To her you said:

"I'd love to spend all my time writing to you; I'd love to share with you all that goes through my mind, all that weighs on my heart, all that gives air to my soul; phantoms of art, dreams that would be so beautiful if they could come true."

The most beautiful character of all was Marta Abba. Actress. Your muse. Your inspiration. This was your great love story, and here you experienced your deepest connection... with the woman who inspired the desperate passion that enveloped you to the end of your days. Together you shared a dream.

What did she symbolize for you, **LUIGI?**

Inspiration? Confidante? Collaborator?

Was her spirited independence a passage to the feminine? More than that, **LUIGI,** she enveloped your world of illusion... was a transition from your battle with reality. She was the myth that kept you connected.

"With all your soul, which rejoices in me and creates inside me that sense of a fable in which all the characters breathe, and the words bloom like flowers that seem astonished at being born."

Wherever you are now, **LUIGI,** your characters are alive. They are your immortality, they flush the imagination, they run wild and free just the way you wanted them to and like you... they go to the limits of their sanity, wrestle with truth, wear their masks, disregard reality.... they are dependent on their disguise, they take their own lives and hide behind their illusions.

Whatever we know of you, **LUIGI,** we know through your characters. They have been loyal to you. A writer creates his world as he creates the moments in his life and in that sense, we are with you forever.

"I present myself to you in a form suitable to the relationship I wish to achieve with you."

DREAMERS

Why does the eye see a thing more clearly in dreams than the imagination when awake?

- Leonardo da Vinci

When I was in my first year of Junior high school...

it was customary to let all the Catholic kids have Wednesday afternoons off to attend catechism.

However...

There was a movie theater directly across from school and the temptation was much too great... so I spent every Wednesday afternoon playing hooky at the local theater.

I sat in the dark theater, dreaming and watching...

A whole new world of imagination opened up to me on the silver screen...

I saw names like Coppola, Magnani, Sinatra, Pacino, Di Niro... names that ended in a vowel just like mine did. And as I sat there in the dark theater, I thought...

"If they could do it, I can do it too."

And in my dreams I always go back to that movie theater in that little Italian ghetto in the Bronx...

Where it all began for me...

Francis Ford Coppola

"Maestro"

Sun in Aries

Director

"If you don't take a risk then how are you going to make something really beautiful, that hasn't been seen before?"

FRANCIS... ASKS,

WHAT IS SOMETHING REALLY BEAUTIFUL? ...and he answers...

To take your dreams and place them in the world to win or lose

Is it simply a wonderful attempt to look for something bigger? Or is there a force in a man that urges him to seek all possibilities... to explore the impossible... to break out of the prison that confines him to a set of rules.

Perhaps, it is all these things together

A risk once taken no longer belongs to you. It has been revealed and the world takes possession. There are men who understand that an artist cannot reach total freedom without taking a risk... and he becomes the man who dares to create the center of his own private universe.

The entire world becomes a seduction

IT TAKES A RISK

"They didn't like the cast. They didn't like the way I was shooting it. I was always on the verge of getting fired."

Paramount had so little faith in Francis Ford Coppola as a filmmaker that they hired another director to follow him around the set of *The Godfather* just to remind him *he could be replaced at any moment.*

As it turned out, Coppola went on to win multiple awards, including an Academy award... the film is preserved in the United States National film Registry and is ranked second on the list of 100 best movies by the American Film Institute. Director Stanley Kubrick believed that *The Godfather* was...

...possibly the greatest movie ever made

"The only risk is to waste your life, so that when you die, you say, 'Oh, I wish I had done this...' I did everything I wanted to do, and I continue to."

FRANCIS,

You always try to discover the moments of life that jump right up at us... that stop us in our tracks so we can feel something... that allow us to seize a new reality or a universal truth... that uncover dimensions of emotional eruption...

...realizing that those are the moments that we never forget

FRANCIS,

You have travelled the ladder of fire... have split the fragments that separate the senses... and have *taken us to different dimensions.*

Life and art are in perpetual movement

They have their own evolution. It is the artist... *the dreamer...* that takes inner visions and allows them to take form... always leaving room for the imagination.

Sharing His Mastery

What was the hardest part, Francis? Was it the beginnings, the endings, the pathos, the living, dying, the struggle, yearning, waiting, searching, wanting?... the master always dies a thousand deaths so that he may live again. The master is schizophrenic, he breaks down into parts, not always certain where he is going, divided, delusional, fragmented.

It is the artist who can put the pieces together again, to awaken the core of the imagination and bring us amazing stories that transform perceptions. The artist explores, dissects complicated systems... and remains outside of convention... always a lonely traveler on his journey.

He finds the places where he can escape tradition and develop his own rules

FRANCIS,

It takes balls to defy the establishment... to govern your by own rules... to take your art on an adventure and to overcome the obstacles.

And who would not love a man who trusts his balls?

Anna Magnani

"Volcano"

Sun in Pisces

Actress

*"When I die,
when people will be thinking of me,
they should know that
Magnani never betrayed them,
and that Magnani never betrayed
herself."*

ANNA,

Who would dare to look into the heart of a volcano?

Was it dangerous to be a woman? To love, ANNA?... Where did it hurt most...

In the darkness?

Love lived only in the moment and brought you to the precipice and there would always be that hunger.

What was it, ANNA, that made you feel like *you were the only one that reached for fire*?

The set is quiet. The lights are turned on. The projector hums and the technicians prepare. A woman steps in front of the cameras. She is dark. Her eyes pierce you like a hallucinogen... vibrant as they explore the very depth of your imagination. She exudes an earthy sexuality ...a magnetic wildness, erotic and sensuous.

She has the seductive power of Michelangelo, Dante, da Vinci, Pirandello, the river Po, the scent of the

Mediterranean, Roma, and Duse... all of which carry the secret windows of the past. Her eyes stare at you like a womb with a thousand embryos.

The Actress

She steps before the camera. Her voice is sultry. She gestures with her hands. A passionate magician becomes obsessed as she transforms herself. There is an untamed, bawdy sensuality, an animal attraction that pulls you toward her. **With her comes an inexorable power.**

The camera rolls

Eyes, illusive and warm, hot and proud... eyes that still haunt us... a drama in anonymity.

Where did their magic come from?

They are not ordinary eyes... their addiction comes to us and somehow we can never measure up to ***...the dare*** ...to pursue life and feel things.

What do you want us to feel, ANNA?

Mountains, **ANNA.** Did you want us to feel mountains? Fragments? Passing things?... things that pass us by as we attempt to squeeze them between our expectations?... Did you want us to feel the woman?... the universal energy that brought you closer to a tempestuous yearning?... We can see it in your eyes. They were the instruments that brought us to the infinite dimensions of being a woman.

It was like living in the parts of the mind where yearning comes alive at its deepest levels.

That is where you lived

Whatever it was you were trying to tell the world, we did not understand and you remained *...untouched* ...on your journey ...with an evolution of fire and passion... with your dark marble eyes and your strange mystique... *feverish...* painted with the color of earth and all your profound moments of solitude. The actress playing all the rituals... the characters wearing your masks and we wonder...

Which one of the disguises were you?

Were there times you could not wait, **ANNA,** for the mystery that lay hidden?... to feel what was there, in the restlessness that took your breath away?

And what about the fire in your eyes?...

Was there enough of the quicksand to challenge your feelings? Did those eyes see everything?

There are things that fascinate us, bring us to a time of greatness when we step out of our hiding place and recognize the impermanency of illusion.

Was it ever enough?

And, in the journey, you travelled alone... profoundly moving, taking you - and us - to places that were once travelled by women of other centuries... where we see their inexorable presence in the corners of your eyes.

They lay in the shadows waiting for you

Did you know, **ANNA** that we are all afraid of being hurt?

Whatever happened to the happy endings?

Roberto Rossellini

"Paisan"

Sun in Taurus

Director

"The great mission of art ought to be to free men from their conditioning."

ROBERTO,

It takes a bold and confident man, living in his personal truth to open the gates to a new cinematic consciousness... a man who stared film history right in the face and gave us...

The "New Movie"

Perhaps it was a way of holding on to that last moment of reality... as though you were part of a very special moment of cinematic history that brought the world a new age of filmmaking.

What is there in a man's spirit that urges him to take a different path?

There is a secret place in the mind that evolves when no one is shaping it... trying to persuade it... condition or conform it.

A mind like that offers the world a kind of freedom that seeks to take things and transform them. It becomes heightened into a new impulse to reality... shedding the old one because it has only one way to go...

Toward expansion without interruption

Art is promiscuous and wild... licentious in its desire for you

It offers you it's goods somewhere in the darkness of your mind... alone in the spaces you have provided... it selfishly wraps itself in the corners of your prose... only to liberate itself.

An artist needs to let her in... let art spread herself... and, in her salacious desire to seduce you, let her take you to that special place that only art can bring you.

Ideas are brief moments in the universe... yet every so often, we capture them and they become a piece of us... and in those moments we can all grow together to form a new reality. It's like giving birth and hearing your child breathe for the very first time.

Some call that evolution

PAISAN

So yours, **ROBERTO...** was the great mission of art... that you could reassure your audience that you were simply filming a significant part of the way things were. You brought a sense of "real time" and humanity to cinema with a unique understanding of the world we live in... and in that sense you have become the spirit of inspiration.

Were you the man that heard the sound of the human impulse?

Your restless soul was never satisfied with unraveling life's mystery. You, **ROBERTO...** found your source in the soul... you, in a sense, invented the soul in cinema... gave it the one dimension it never had, took it one step beyond it's limits. It was a kind of madness... a fierce belief that you could transform a system... and in your way you remade the world of film because you believed you could.

"I am always for the crazy people." You said.

THE LETTER

Dear Mr. Rossellini,

I saw your films Open City and Paisan, and enjoyed them very much. If you need a Swedish actress who speaks English very well, who has not forgotten her German, who is not very understandable in French, and who in Italian knows only "ti amo," I am ready to come and make a film with you.

Ingrid Bergman

I AM READY! I will leave my husband and come to Italy...
Then came the international scandal!

Yet, what is a scandal? Is it, as a culture, that we cannot accept it when someone steps beyond the social boundaries of what we have determined is our value system? Is it when we cannot accept anything that is unorthodox, unfamiliar?... And in some ways, is it not inevitable to those who step out of conventional morals to be sacrificed?...

It was rumored that it was a woman who got you interested in filmmaking in the first place. Yes, there were women. There was Marcelina, your first wife... there was Anna Magnani, Ingrid Bergman and Sonaki.

"I always keep an open window," he said in his relationships with women.

There will always be those who venture beyond the frontiers... who create new directions... who dare to explore unknown territories... those who will make sweeping movements, innovations and exceed expectations... and those who make extraordinary flights of humanity because there is greatness in their courage.

ROBERTO, for all that is said and done... for your love of life, art, and women... that makes you a fellow countryman in any language.

Paisan

Eleanora Duse

"Fata Morgana"

Sun in Libra

Actress

"If the sight of the blue skies fills you with joy, if the simplest things of nature have a message that you understand, rejoice, for your soul is alive."

ELEANORA.

Sometimes, in the morning after a cold night, you can look out over the horizon... and see something happening in the sky... perhaps you look at it in wonder because you are not certain what you will find... it becomes an integral part of a powerful attraction.

Someone has evoked the secrets of magic and has created a mystical experience

There is a haze, a shadowy reflection as though you have entered a mysterious region. The scent of roses fill the air. A surreal vision overcomes you, the world seems watery... and you feel a sense of supremacy. You move past your limitations and wonder at the perception of your own mind. Who is there?

A Sorceress perhaps?

A sorceress who possesses telepathy of words... of movements... and can contact you from great distances. Her magic can conquer emotions, the spirit and unleash your hidden secret thoughts. She can look you in the eyes and see into the vast inner spaces of your mind... and there, at that moment... teleport great emotion and characterizations...

Close your eyes

Feel the breath of something that will confront your imagination...

Something magnificent is about to happen

Ghosts... summoning images as though distances are gone. What are the ghosts?

Are they time itself?

So beautiful is the figure of a great actress, **ELEANORA**... it lights up the world with ecstasy. She emits a strange and compelling rhythm like a force of nature... dark wide eyes... the color of sable... *rebellious*... **she creates** something that rises above the ordinary... that follows its own journey... that is impatiently alive and sweeps across the stage.

There, in that moment, a legend was created

Your legend **ELEANORA**...

There exists in great moments an incomparable experience... There is a new pattern... a new model is sculptured out of the old. An intersection cannot be crossed without the template for a new awareness. That is what change brings. A new door is opened.

In a time such as this the imagination is confronted, a spirit drives the uninhibited forces of a Dionysian like a magnet that frees the soul... where the senses are gratified.

ELEANORA, was your passion enough? Did the dreams in your eyes and the boldness of your sensuality take you where you meant to go?... like lightning to the illusion? Was it enough?... the seduction of the theatre, the pull of stage lights, the feel of motion and intensity... the insight of character, the unending adulation of art, the thousand voices inside you, the piercing and fierce emotion of the actress, the delirious sound of the words, the creation... **ELEANORA,** the creation...

Was it all enough?

"If the sight of the blue skies fills you with joy," you said, *"if the simplest of nature have a message that you understand, rejoice, for your soul is alive."*

And then there was Venice

THE PROMISE OF PISA

Yes, there was Venice and the lust for your art. Venice with its romance and the sun at dusk and the quiet nights and the hunger to dream. Venice, with the cultivated intellectualism... Venice, with its secret waterways and lagoons and arches and canals and the fire in the sky at sunset casting a glow over the city.

Or was it the intimacy of Venice in the early morning which sunk into your imagination... which spread across your sky?... Was it the palatial wonders and how the sun reflects on the water? Venice where the mind escapes, and where you provoked your body and gave it the gift of love.

d'Annunzio

How did he come to you? Is that where you abandoned yourself? What did you see in him? In d'Annunzio? Was he a mirror where you saw yourself?

Or was he merely an illusion of an ideal?

"Is it perhaps because the heart is like the sea," you said, "I don't know---I don't know anymore. I swear that I don't know anymore."

What did anyone know, **ELEANORA?** What did they know about the temple where you came to worship... what did they know about standing alone with imagination filling your senses and transcending time. You said it all through your characters. They said it for you. That was your element of creation, there in the light with the curtains drawn.

That was the world where your heart spoke

There are words to speak that come from another source, from the profundity of the soul. Wasn't that your secret, **ELEANORA?**... A place that has no fear and is born of instinct and impulse and rebellion.

The stage has an eminence and like love, it is obsessive... it is impossible to satisfy and is always hungry, wanting more... *insatiable*... ravenous.

And what about D'Annunzio?

Could he compare to the wild, trembling fever... the intoxicating seduction that filled your mind like a drug when you stood in front of an audience? You could hear them breathing in the dark, see your reflection in their eyes... feel them shifting in their seats. A narcotic. An electric pulse.

Could anything compare to this feeling?

You belonged to another world, one divided by a curtain that opened and closed. This was the place where you disappeared each night...

And where you found yourself

And what were you to him? To d'Annunzio... a wanderer moved by dreams?... Someone to bring fame to his words...

You were his muse

What was between you? The commitment between two artists... something bigger than love?... The cord that bound you was dedication to your art... The promise of a dream made you an entity that was complete and with that you envisioned a new art, a new theatre...

"I have found the harmony," **you wrote to d'Annunzio.**

Sometimes, contracts, like hearts get broken...

And so it was with her.

"He has squeezed me like a lemon," you cried, *"and then thrown me away."*

ELEANORA,

You were a woman that did not conform to what the world of art expected. You were moved by your own intelligence and stubborn sensuality. You will be remembered as a woman who went to the mountaintop, looked over the peaks and hills and passed through the shadows.

And when the cold nights came and the rain turned chill... and your heart ached with the endless search for love and art... you became the lightning... with it's light that reaches out across continents.

"When we grow old," you said, "there can only be one regret... not to have given enough of ourselves."

And for you, ELEANORA,

There are no regrets...

LOVERS

Any time not spent on love is wasted.

-Torquato Tasso

Now, there's a thought.

Love

You might think that Italians invented the word. What with Casanova, Rudolf Valentino, Sofia Loren and the voice of Frank Sinatra.

However, what I learned about love from being Italian is that love is an attitude.

My mother's door was always open for whoever needed comforting

My mother always had time to listen to her friends when they needed someone to hear them.

I will never forget my mother staying up late at night sewing me a costume for when I danced in the streets...

...From the streets to the stage and my mother sitting in the first row while I was dancing... rooting for me...

That's what she taught me about love...

Rudolf Valentino

"male sex symbol"

Sun in Taurus

Movie idol

"Women are not in love with me but with the picture of me on the screen.

I am merely the canvas on which women paint their dreams."

DEAR RODOLFO ALFONSO RAFFAELLO PIERRE FILIBERT GUGLIELMI DI VALENTINA D'ANTOGUOLLA,

I'll call you Rudy, if that's okay with you

I think of your glossy black luminous hair... racy sideburns and red formidable lips... **dark penetrating eyes...** a passionate touch of your hands, a smoldering kiss... and the wild and provoking image of your style that sent women screaming and crying.

The world was invited to fall into your arms

That was you, **RUDOLF VALENTINO,** living on the periphery of an immensely powerful intimacy... The legacy of a great lover locked into an erotic frenzy of lightening impulses... *adoration...* You lived in the darkest corners of the most prurient desires...

In forbidden fantasy

Was it enough, Rudy?

What could you do with all that adulation?

Even those who questioned your masculinity... the force that brought you into the arena of loving... both women and men... even they yielded to your erotic power... as though you were...

A flame simmering with life force

"If I choose, I can make you love me." He said.

Is that what it was about? Love? Sometimes love has its own rules. It requires nutrients and extremes and often creates its own world. Had you been left with only the fragments?

Did you waken to the sound of breathing in the night? Soft breasts, thighs, flesh. Did it matter whose genitals were in your hands just as long as you felt something? Isn't that what you wanted, **RUDY**, to feel that close, warm, breathing... a heart beating close to yours...

Rudy, were you hurt?

You were a genuine, full-fledged dream...

You were so close to your own darkness... where lived a sense of the forbidden... a soft, undulating comfort.

You represented an awakening of the senses... *wild with fantasy...* a new hunger for the ideal experience... the revealing of the secret hidden places waiting to be touched... the freeing of compulsive and excessive instinct...

What did it take from you, RUDY...

You who had so much adulation?... Could you recognize the impetus for an early death?...

"A studio, the glaring lights, the hammering of the carpenters, the noise and smell of it all—THAT is really home!"

You were the illusive miracle

Even as your public clung to you... you were the lover separated from the adventure because, after all... *you were an invention...* Your image gave the world... for a moment, something to believe in.

There was a dream of your slow, warm embrace... an elaborate jeweled flower opening their petals... a golden rod between the legs that became immortal.

"The public expects me to be one of the romantic heroes I play on the screen, and the real Valentino isn't one bit like that."

Was it all a performance? Were they all Dante's Beatrice?

What was it like in the dark?

Could you tell the difference?... if it was a man or a woman - or was it merely a chance to love?... *Perhaps it was a way to immortalize the symbol...* Was it unspeakable?... *the earth trembling...* did the symbol become your sanctuary?... did the symbol transform from Dionysian lover to the naked, forbidden and all consuming womb?

You see... **RUDY...**

It is a treacherous path...

First there is desire... desire that comes like a breath of opium... hands on the breasts... voluptuous, soft... burning its way into the flesh... bringing everything closer. A kind of silence comes... as the complexities of love sort themselves out. Then the moments explode into each other like an erupting volcano... and this emotional lava can lead to... *liberation*...

A man, after all, comes to you in the night with kisses... he overwhelms the senses. Is that the way it was? The night spiraling with imagination?...

Because that's what love is.

It is always waiting for the beginning to never end

It was said your lovemaking had been so wild that a woman went into a cataleptic fit.

A cataleptic fit? Really? Honestly? For sure?

Sooooooo---what do you say, **RUDY....**

Your place or mine?

Marta Abba

"liberator"

Sun in Cancer

Actress

Muse for Pirandello

"The work was the fruit of collaboration, that of two spirits united by the same love - the love for each other through their higher love for art"

MARTA,

Imagine a Greek Goddess inspired by the songs of Sophocles, Euripides and Sappho. It is summer... the time for love, and you are surrounded by music and dance. Imagine gnarled trunks of olive trees and leafy branches swaying in the warm breeze.

Imagine mountains in the distance... fertile pockets of rich dark soil between rocks where grapes grow for wine... Feel the quiet love of a goddess... a mistress of the winds... a goddess with the power to bestow great imagination to artists...

Imagine you can hear the soft waves of the Mediterranean Sea as it drifts toward the shore... evoking dreams and a sense of warmth and excitement. Imagine that you carry this gift of the goddess with you in your travels... it is yours...

You are the goddess and you sing for only those that you choose hear your song

NOW, Imagine you are the muse for one of the most prolific writers of the twentieth century...

That you are the source of his greatest truths...

MARIA, you were 25 years old when you met Luigi Pirandello who was 58. But what do years matter when a man is obsessed with the fragment of an image that mirrored his soul?...

YOU *were the illumination*

YOU were an independent spirit who touched the glory of a poet. An actress who conquered Broadway in one evening... and became the lead for Pirandello... who wrote plays for you.

But who were YOU? The muse for Pirandello? The actress? When you entered Pirandillo's life... you brought with you your concern for female emancipation. You were the catalyst for him to create forceful female characters in his plays... plays where women were portrayed as real people...

MARIA, you were more than a muse... you became his collaborator and enhanced his creative genius. You brought him the feminine... you helped overcome the divisions between male and female...

One cannot give birth without the other

That was your time, **MARTA**... you were somewhere between reality and illusion. You lived in the center of Pirandello's obsession... and yet...

Could the world be trusted to understand?

Love, **MARTA,** it was all about love... The visceral languages of senses, and emotion... the dance of creation. It was about the most important aspect of being an actress... *to be daring...* to risk one's world and to submit only to art.

Imagine a life that lives the adventure of dreams

You were not an ordinary muse, **MARTA**. Your invocation brought 'the feminine' to the seat of creation... built bridges... brought the female closer to the source.

You went on to form your own company and you continued to perform plays for your mentor. You set the muse free so she could become her own instrument of creation... *changing dynamics...* because imagination never ceases and freedom is always the journey.

Is that the secret of the muse?

Giacomo Casanova

"Adventurer"

Sun in Aries

Lover

Seducer

"As for women, I have always found that the one I was in love with smelled good, and the more copious her sweat the sweeter I found it."

CASANOVA,

The seed once planted blossomed

Its fertile passage became a rebirth... a rebirth rich with adoration, temptation and magic. The nurtured fruit was devoured....

It was the aphrodisiac of eternal lust and temptation.

It was summertime when Eve plucked the forbidden apple from the tree, because that is the time for love. There must have been a kind of mystical mastery that overwhelmed her... and she felt sweet, voluptuous and ripe. What had awakened within her such pleasurable power? She must have felt an infinite softness and a quiet acquiesce.

Once tasted, the apple became an instrument of seduction and sensual beauty and she could no longer resist. She bit deep into the red apple.

The taste was succulent and warm... profound and inherently exciting. Within its pulpy substance was the very core of promise... and for centuries it has been the symbol of temptation and desire.

Then came the ancient serpent with its mythological fire... biting its way through the darkness... bringing with it a sense of immortality... for it is indeed the giver of eternal pleasure.

CASANOVA, you said, *"I don't conquer, I submit."*

You were an adventurer, a soldier, spy, diplomat, author, poet... yet, your reputation will always rest on being the world's most prolific lover... Was it submission after all?

Were you the first to make love an art?

First you marked your target. Then a smile, a small gesture with the eyes... *come closer...* And then the touch...

Is that how it began for you, CASANOVA, with that touch? Did your body language leave something for the imagination? You moved slowly, waiting for the desire to catch up with you.

Perhaps you brought her flowers. Roses. Red ones. The color of passion. Red that stimulates the senses, emotionally intense. You can hear her heart beat. Red is hot and dangerous... suggesting a hint of sin, forbidding romance and the power of love.

Did you kiss her hand? Perhaps you lingered awhile until you both felt the magic. What were their secrets? Each woman has her own rhythm... her own fragrance. They kept you in orbit, spinning around until you felt the spirit of their sensuality.

In a sense you felt you were the one submitting to their whims. You had seized the immensity of the moment, giving yourself to that which was unattainable and it became your greatest triumph.

Somehow you were able to produce a world of fragments.

Did their fragrance intoxicate you?

There was always room for one more. How extraordinary to be part of something so overwhelming, so ruled by instinct... that being so close to the flesh could be mythological.

And yet, we will always wonder, what was it really like? The scandals, the exploits, the sexual conquests, the adventure and the women, yes, the chambermaids, actresses, noblewomen, nymphomaniacs and yes, even a few nuns. Man, after all, is a creature of instinct... he is strong and lives his life searching for the unattainable.

But did you know, Casanova, that your kisses were making history?

HEROES And HEROINES

The darkest places in hell are reserved for those who maintain their neutrality in times of moral crisis.

--Dante Alighieri

When Italians first came to this country there was much prejudice.

I remember when I was eight years old... playing in the city pool, someone looked at me and said...

"you have the map of Italy all over your face"

And I ran to hide because I thought it meant I was really ugly...

But, we had our heroes too

Nicola Sacco & Bartolomeo Vanzetti

"I would not wish to a dog or to a snake what I have had to suffer for things that I am not guilty of. But my conviction is that I have suffered for things that I am guilty of. I am suffering because I am a radical and indeed I am a radical; I have suffered because I was an Italian, and indeed I am an Italian; I have suffered more for my family and my beloved than for myself; but I am so convinced to be right that if you could execute me two times, and if I could be reborn two other times, I would live again to do what I have done already." -Vanzetti

But what good is the evidence and what good is the argument? They are determined to kill us regardless of evidence, of law, of decency, of everything. If they give us a delay tonight, it will only mean they will kill us next week. Let us finish tonight. I'm weary of waiting seven years to die, when they know all the time they intend to kill us."

-Sacco, August 22, 1927, fifteen hours before he and Vanzetti were executed.

Sacco-Taurus
Vanzetti-Gemini

Political prisoners/Executed August 22, 1927

SACCO AND VANZETTI

In 1927 a journalist wrote, "Do you know what chance a colored boy has down South to get a square deal? Well, an Italian in Massachusetts has **just about the same kind of a chance** to get a square deal on the charge of murder."

While storm warnings were ordered from Eastport to Nantucket...

Babe Ruth hit his 40th homer, President Coolidge was visiting Yellowstone park, the radio was playing *"I'm looking over a four leaf clover that I overlooked before"*... a man was killed in a street at Port au port... the International Paper Company agreement passed second reading and, in an atmosphere of fear that communists, socialists, anarchists and immigrants would overthrow the American scene, Sacco and Vanzetti sat in a small jail ...

Waiting to die at midnight on August 22, 1927...

NICOLO AND BARTOLOMEO, what was it about you that captured the pulse of an entire world? Was it about the innocence we have lost?... that place inside us that we have reserved, kept quiet... that we had not intended to confront? Had innocence become a kind of perversion?... something we sacrificed in order to replenish the powers of a cultural establishment?

Was this about Justice? Or was it fear?

Had fear become a kind of justification that sacrificed the spirit?

Every once in a while something comes along that pulls at the soul of a nation and we can no longer remain silent. Fear bites at us from the inside... scarring us as we remain bottled up and frozen... *divided...*

Does this inner conflict affect our dreams?... this battle where conscience surrenders to establishment... Is the status quo something to believe in?... We had a chance to confront intolerance... to escape... *free and untamed...*

In the meantime... A large angry crowd gathered.... The smell of fumes coming from the smokestacks surrounding the prison permeated the air... Two men were put to death in a narrow room.... and the lights dimmed on that tragic morning.

What was it like to know you are going to die?

Did you wonder about tomorrow and what it will be like without you? Did you watch the sun from your small window and realize that life can be lived only in the moment?...

The last words of Bartolomeo Vanzetti.

"If it had not been for these things, I might have lived out my life talking at street corners to scorning men. I might have died, unmarked, unknown, a failure. Now we are not a failure. This is our career and our triumph. Never in our full life could we hope to do such work for tolerance, for justice, for man's understanding of man as now we do by accident. Our words--our lives--our pains--nothing! The taking of our lives--lives of a good shoemaker and a poor fish-peddler--all! That last moment belongs to us--that agony is our triumph."

Governor Michael Dukakis proclaimed August 23rd Sacco and Vanzetti Memorial Day fifty years after their execution. *"Any stigma and disgrace shall be forever removed from their names...."* he declared... The trial proceedings had been *"permeated by prejudice against foreigners and hostility toward unorthodox political views."* Dukakis did not speak to Sacco and Vanzetti's guilt or innocence, but he acknowledged that the men had paid with their lives for being radicals and aliens.

So what do we do with the hours we have remaining?... Do we let the wind take us where we are going?...

Or do we shake the winds of change?

Vanzetti-1918

Tina Modotti
"the Language of Roses"

Sun in Leo

Photographer

"I cannot solve the problem of life by losing myself in the problem of art."

TINA

What becomes of a rose that's been plucked from the garden?

Velvety petals secluded in a spectrum of color and fragrance... reminding us of summer... **TINA**, *the rose*... whose nucleus holds the mystery of existence... an aphrodisiac sprinkling petals wherever they may fall. How quickly and easily your petals reflect beauty... yet with a sense of destiny and fate... because all things must die.

You were a symbolic center of mystery and secrets... that spoke in the language of roses... the language of lovers, adventurers, artists... the language of intense passion as though the flesh had its own perceptions.

There is something celestial that happens when the sun reflects on a rose... where every second counts as the sun goes down... because there is only one moment when a rose shares its fragrance to anyone passing by.

The Notorious Tina Modotti

No matter how broken the world gets, there are always those who want to put it back together again.

You were an actress... a passionate revolutionary, a great beauty, and a lover... and like the essence of the rose ...*a mystery*. And what did you do with the abundance **TINA**?... What did you do with the passion that could not wait and the intensity you needed to fulfill a powerful life?

What happens to the things that cannot wait until tomorrow?

TINA, you needed to fly... to conquer that necessity... and I wonder if you ever wakened from the dream... from the fire that prevailed over you.

What was behind those dark eyes that looked far beyond the lens of the camera? The storm that followed you, the wind that carried you through the labyrinth and gave you refuge?... the splintered promises?...

You said: *"this, and no other, was my place and that I had to take very direct and immediate action as a revolutionary."*

Sometimes you stood in the paroxysm of your dream

"I cannot accept life as it is ---it is too chaotic---too unconscious---therefore my resistance to it---I am forever struggling to mold life according to my temperament and need---in other words I put too much art in my life---too much energy, and consequently I have not much left to give to art."

The Hopeless Rebel

You were sitting with your roots in the warm earth... Did you throw it all away, **TINA**... for the quest for transcendence? So the artist could surrender to the rebel? Was that it? **TINA**, what were you without your song?... an empty space where lived your art. Did you hide behind the camera?

"I am an antifascist because I am an enemy of tyrannies."

You put it all aside for the revolution... with your heart open and your imperturbable kindness... and you decided you could never quit, never leave the broken pieces behind...

And you learned to breathe in the fire

You turned in your camera... for the revolution.

The revolution. It hasn't come yet...

TINA. You said,
"Long life to your work---it is the only thing which never fails you."

Vito Marcantonio

"quintessential man"

Sun in Sagittarius

Congressman

"You only live once and it is best to live one's life with one's conscience rather than to temporize or accept with silence those things one believes to be against the interests of one's people and one's nation."

VITO,

What is it like to be inside the wind?...

Forever circling... sweeping in like a tsunami?

A mind like yours is mercurial, capricious... and sometimes creates a tidal wave of such enormous dimensions... so compelling that we are forced to give it relevance... We are filled with a sense of optimism... and tremendous power...

You **VITO MARCANTONIO**... *urban maverick...* were that wave... that tsunami. You lived all your working hours in the dream you belonged to. The rhythm of the streets was your mantra... the immigrants, poverty... the wild and boisterous sounds the wind made as you rushed into your orbit... were all part of the adventure.

Could you have done it all?

The mad attempt to fight the system... defending civil rights and the workingman... and the constant struggle to transform politics?

"I fully realize, " you said, " that men must pay the great price in order to adhere to ideals. I fully realize that one needs guts to pursue such a course..."

And guts you had, Vito

How many streets did you walk down to find the same scattered silences, the same empty eyes staring back at you... the same exaggerated disappointments and contradictions... the same paradoxes. How much of you got lost in the complexity of the indigence that abounded on Ninety Sixth Street to one hundred and Twenty-fifth Street... from Lexington Avenue to the East River?...

Who were they?...

These Italians, Puerto Ricans, Jews, and African Americans? How much of yourself did you see in them?... such that you could not let go? Perhaps this was your way of affirming life... a way of freeing yourself from your past.

East Harlem was your mirror, a place where you could abandon yourself. It was a place where you joined the gamut of human life... life which reflected the very essence of who you are.

You were all part of the same fabric

VITO MARCANTONIO... *fighter for the underprivileged...*

And when you felt most alone... surrounded by great opposition... that's when you fought the hardest. That was when you remained true to yourself... You lived most deeply when you faced the onslaught.

"I vote my conscience." You said.

And indeed you did, Congressman...

You, **VITO**, have passed through your transitions nobly... and the triumph of your ideals is stamped in history.

There are times when greatness becomes visible and it lives for a while. It has a moment in the sun and becomes luminous... and we have no choice but to let it dazzle us... and then it slips away... leaving us in a state of reverence.

The streets were your home, **VITO**, your Mecca to defend. But you had a rendezvous with destiny, didn't you? And on that rainy day in New York City, your heart made an inevitable and uncompromising conquest. You lost the battle. They found you on the very streets you loved...

The streets that finally claimed you

Oriana Fallaci

"partisan"

Sun in Cancer

Journalist/Writer

"I have always looked on disobedience toward the oppressive as the only way to use the miracle of having been born."

ORIANA,

The open sky is a place for wings

Some people live there. The sky is not for everyone. It is an anchor for those who have not invented a disguise and are willing to let us see who they really are. Freedom is the arrogant awakening that dominates a life that dares to confront itself. Once you have tasted the nectar of freedom there is no turning back.

"...If you have wings, you can enjoy flying under sky and in air, and birds know the taste of freedom."

Is that what made you confrontational, controversial and as one biographer called you ***"the greatest political interviewer of modern times"***? You covered war and revolution and were not afraid to refer to ***"those bastards who decide our lives,"*** Your interview with Khomeini went something like this:

FALLACI - "I still have to ask you a lot of things. ***About the chador***, for example, which I was obliged to wear to come and interview you, and which you impose on Iranian women. I am not only referring to the dress but to what it represents, I mean ***the apartheid*** Iranian women have been forced into after the revolution.

They cannot study at the university with men, they cannot work with men, they cannot swim in the sea or in a swimming pool with men. They have to do everything separately, wearing their chador."

khomeini - "None of this concerns you, our customs do not concern you. If you don't like the Islamic dress you are not obliged to wear it, since it is for young women and respectable ladies."

FALLACI - "This is very kind of you, Imam, since you tell me that, I'm going to immediately rid myself of this stupid medieval rag. There!"

What was it like for you **ORIANA**, to have been a partisan during World War II and join the resistance movement... despite your 14 years? You have been a war correspondent, a journalist, you have written for leading newspapers... and you were even shot three times during the 1968 Tlatelolco massacre... dragged by the hair and left for dead.

A Man

Then it happened during one of your interviews.

Alexandros Panagoulis

You fell in love. He was like you, wasn't he? Courageous, provocative... Did you experience a kind of spiraling that filtered through you? Love is warm in a cold world, **ORIANA**, and there must have been many moments when you breathed fire. Love is like that, yet... your life has taught you there is no such thing as permanence.

A man who fought with the Greek resistance against the 1967 dictatorship of Georgios Papadopoulos... and made an unsuccessful attempt to assassinate him, Alexandros was captured and.... *when he died*... You maintained that he was assassinated by the remnants of the Greek military... and you wrote a book about him. ...*A Man*

"Alekos Panagoulis, the man I loved, was killed. From the moment Alekos died, I left journalism, shut myself in my country house and started a book about him."

A Woman

A woman who dared to do great things, who has known passion and sweetness. A woman who has known power... has walked in shadows... who opened new doors transcending the labyrinth... and looked beyond the limits of an aimless rebellion.

A woman who kept alliances with truth and gave them to the world on her terms and set her own boundaries. A woman that stepped out of the status quo to be led only by the inspiration of her soul.

A woman in her beautiful, mysterious femininity... warm and connected to the universe, never shrinking from her vision, always loyal to her consciousness and yet... there were moments when her heart would break because she was, after all ...*truly human*... there were times when her love and independence challenged ...*everything.*

ORIANA, The day came when you summed it all up and recognized that the time you spent here with us was the right moment... you will be remembered for your courage... for covering wars and revolutions... confronting the leaders of the world... Abrasive and insightful, you will be remembered for your tenacity, abrasiveness, combativeness... your temper and for never betraying your truth.

Take it or leave it.

You said,

"I leave shreds of my soul on every experience."

OUTCASTS

I do not feel obliged to believe

that the same God who has

endowed us with sense, reason,

and intellect has intend us to forgo

their use -

--Galileo Galilei

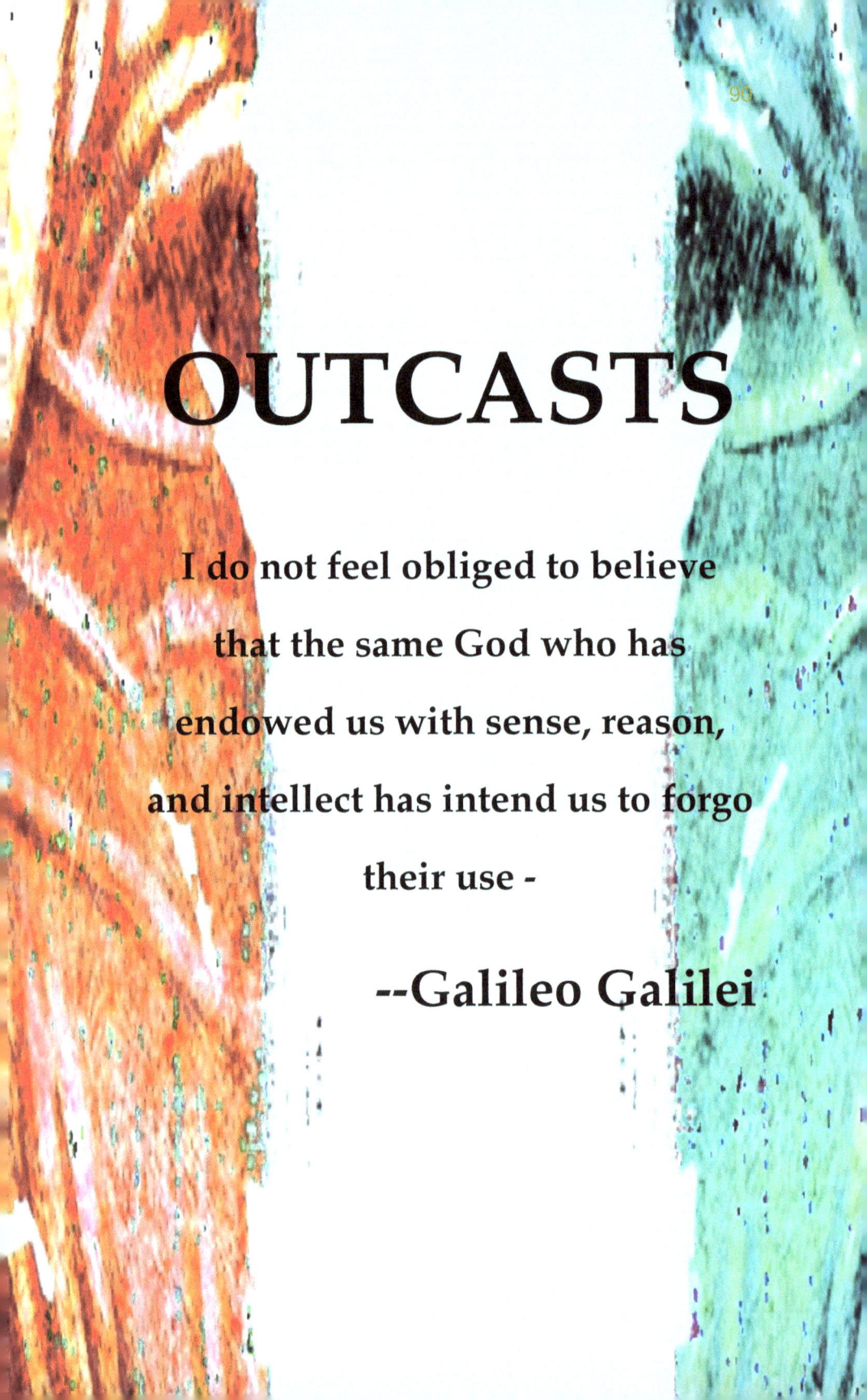

Italians forever live under the shadow of the Mafia...

No matter how hard we try not to...

We have doctors, lawyers, artists, politicians... and yet, we still face the onslaught. So, you might wonder, why am I including a Mafia legend?

When I was younger and found myself in a frightening situation I had a standard line I used to protect myself. I said,

"My Uncle Louie is not going to like this."

Of course, it sounded like a threat that my Uncle Louie would 'take you out' if you hurt me. That always worked for me and I used it into my adult life...

The truth is **I never had an Uncle Louie**... But, hey, thanks to Uncle Louie anyway!

When I read about Maria Licciardi I realized... here is a brilliant women who, with a swing of the pendulum, could have been a powerful leader in society... a CEO of a large corporation... maybe even...

Prime Minister of her country

Maria Licciardi

"badasssssss"

Sun in Aries

Boss of Bosses Mafia

Head of the Licciardi clan

It was said of her.

"Signora Licciardi is a true 'madrina' (godmother), absolutely,"

La Madrina...

Naples lies between two volcanic regions... Mount Vesuvius and the Phlegraean Fields.

Yet, there was another volcano about to erupt

It began in Secondigliano... gritty, tenements, poverty, and high unemployment... with the slum-like housing developments that sit on the northern edge of Naples. A city rife with social problems... truancy, dropouts, drugs... where the Mafia had infiltrated... A combat zone filled with gangs battling for a bigger share of the loot.

It was said of Secondigliano that, *"people have the culture of the Camorra in their bones."*

They tell us, **MARIA LICCIARDI**... *head of the Camorra family...* that you had ruthless magnetism and did everything on your terms. You craved power, not fame. You were the undisputed boss of the Camorra when your husband and two brothers were arrested. You reigned from 1993 to your arrest in 2001.

You brought together one of the most powerful coalitions of the Camorra clan.

Girl Power

Maria Licciardi brought terror to the streets of Naples.

What is it like to gun down another person, holding a weapon... your hand on the trigger, wielding so much power?

"She's in prison, but she still commands. Prisons don't represent a barrier for the Camorra," a local policeman once said.

Is there a moment of intimacy when you look into the eyes of your victim and revel in their helplessness?... Is there a sense of communion?... Do you become obsessed with the connection?... Do you defy loneliness?... as though some kind of force has tied you together... and you know that in order to live, the other person must die?...

Do you surrender to the moment and feel a sense of freedom?

Do you feel the weight of the gun, **MARIA**, the cold steel heavy in your hand... a servant... an instrument of power?

What do you see at that last moment?... The darkness in their eyes... a desolate stillness... something of yourself perhaps... a bridge to your own obscurity as though without this moment your power would diminish?... Yes, **MARIA**, you have broken the glass ceiling but there is not much rejoicing in that...

When we look at you, we are fascinated by the very thing we reject.

Face to face...

There is something that draws us to you. Something aloof and cold.

The killer inside all of us...

Yes, we kill things. We kill the things we love... we kill animals and we kill our dreams, our hopes, and ourselves. We kill our happiness... *relationships...* we kill the very planet we live on. We start wars and kill some more.

Are we so different then, Maria?

We bury our vulnerabilities and hide behind masks made of stone. We live by our own secret codes. We don't trust each other and we build clans to support our beliefs. We create prisons inside of us and indict ourselves to a life sentence. We seek agreement and banish those who don't agree with us. We are both the accuser and prosecutor. We fight for dominance and crown the conquerors. We don't tolerate people who are different then us.

So-- **MARIA**, *can you make me an offer I can't refuse?*

Aradia

"la strega"

Sun in Leo

Italian witch

Confronting Christian priests she said:

"I rebuke you and I cast you out because you teach punishment and shame to those who would free themselves from the slavery of the church."

ARADIA.

Do you know about fire?

Have you been kissed by the wind?... Have you seen how the moon lights up the sky?... Have you ever been caught between shadows?... Have you felt the mystery in darkness?

The woods were quiet

There was a strange hush, not even a leaf stirred. The moon appeared fixed and the stars clung to the night sky. There was the fragrance of rose buds and lilacs and the smell of incense. The moon was full. There was a virgin stillness and the light of dreams offering radiance to whomever took the journey. There was comfort all around and a luminousness appeared in the distance as the skies opened... when suddenly a voice was heard stirring among the trees and... the night came alive and everything was suddenly turned free.

The trees swayed to the rhythm of her voice... the birds sang to the life of her image... the moon rolled in the sky making room for the stars... and at the stroke of midnight she came.

La Strega

ARADIA DE TOSCANO THE HOLY STREGA,

You were the first witch of the modern world... and you appeared in the fourteenth century in medieval Italy. You brought back...

the Old Religion...

After centuries of rule by Christianity... you awakened it from the ashes of silence.

You challenged the order of things... and gave hope to those who were oppressed. You brought the...

Wisdom of women...

The knowledge that women must be free... that the world must be naked... and that there shall be dancing and singing and music and celebration. Lustrous joyous color returned to the night...

Astral energy reentered the realm... transformations began to flow...

You had a way of listening to your inner voice... even as a child as you sat among the hills near...

The temple of Diana...

It was there that you learned your spirit sense... and to look at the world from a place of illumination.

Goddesses are made of wonder, truth and liberation.

They solve mysteries and they challenge the dark places... They make everything frivolous and sweet with enough warm air to fill the world with imagination.

Your wisdom had become legend...

For you were sent to earth with a quest for all women who have faced themselves... who have confronted their fears and have transcended the past... who have prepared themselves to live with the gifts of the spirit... and...

Accept love in all the ways that it comes

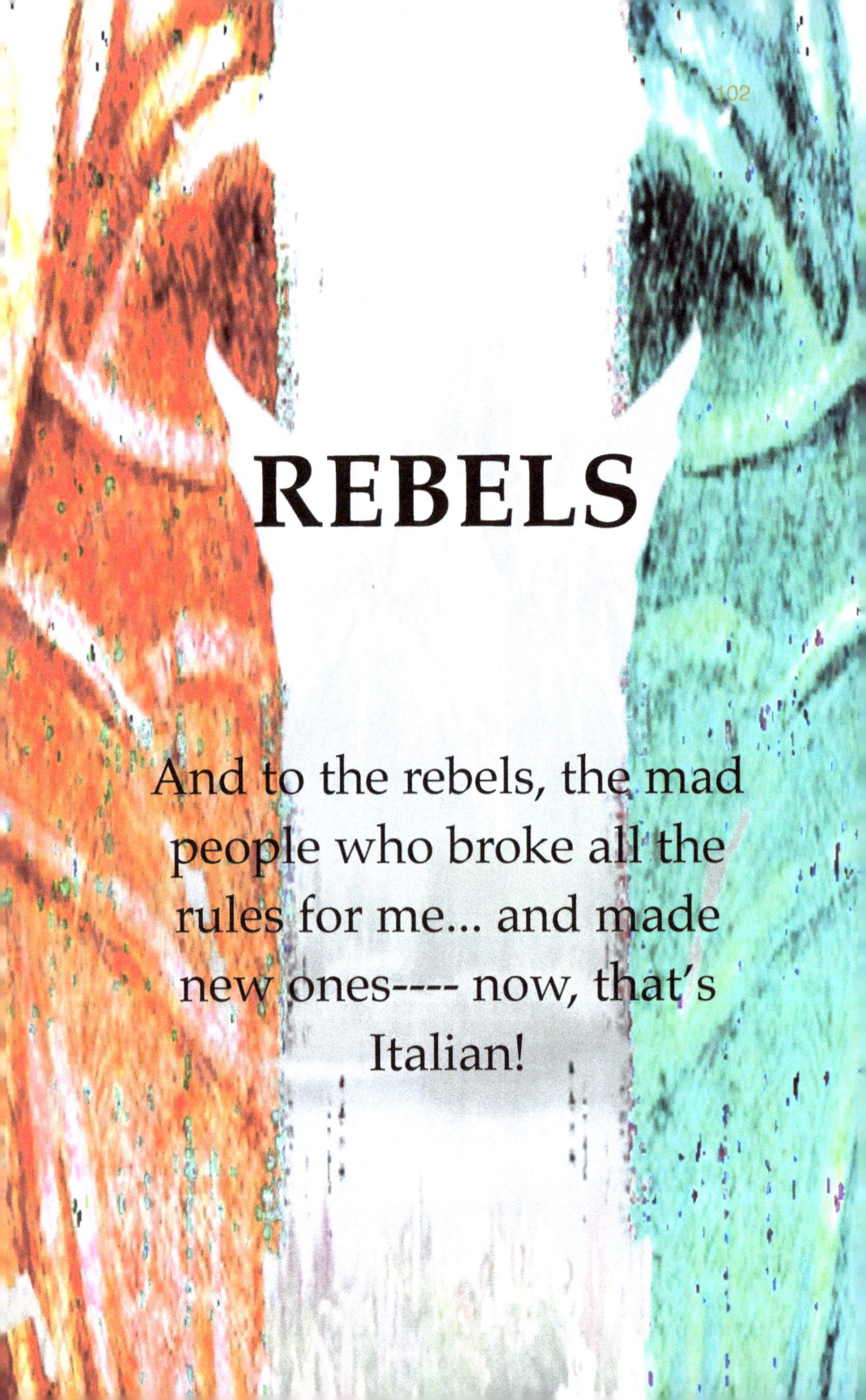

REBELS

And to the rebels, the mad people who broke all the rules for me... and made new ones---- now, that's Italian!

DEAR FRANK,

1915. Little Italy.
What was it like to be born in Hoboken, New Jersey?

Little Italy was the worst side of town. "Guinea Town"... where the aroma of hanging baccala', mozzarella and garlic permeated the streets... The ghosts of Italian immigrants wandered through old barber shops, bakeries, and pizza parlors... streets gangs rumbled. Italian families were seen as dirty and stupid ...*criminal suspects.* Hoboken... a town that made a rough impact on your life....

"When I was there, I just wanted to get the hell out," Sinatra once said of the town where he was born. *"It took me a long time to realize how much of it I took with me."*

There you were, **FRANK**... laying on the table... a newborn infant thought dead. Your grandmother picked you up, stuck you under cold water... you took your first breath... and that's where it all began.

Your Way

Your traumatic birth scarred you

"They weren't thinking of me," **you said,** *"just about my mother. They just ripped me out and tossed me aside."*

The kids taunted you in school ... called you "scarface"... what wound did they give you?

Or, your mother, Dolly... with her wild, explosive displays of dominance... What did that give you?... What did you inherit?

Your childhood brought you a sense of loneliness... and you made the decision to get to a place where you would never be lonely again.

You wrote your own myth

A man who feels weak will strengthen himself... will find power in order to affirm himself... or he will fold. You gave yourself the license to prevail... to triumph over fragility. You did so... you voiced mastery... and attained widespread adoration.

What Was it?

What happens when fear becomes a part of who you are?... when your childhood is filled with powerless effects in the shadow of a strong, domineering mother?... When you dodge the tough kids in the streets... the ones who laughed at the clothes you wore... and tears are quick and common...

Then there are the myths about you and the mob...

They say the police in Naples found a gold cigarette case in the home of Lucky Luciano with an inscription that read, "To my dear pal Lucky, from his friend, Frank Sinatra." They say Sam Giancana wore a sapphire ring that was a gift from you. There are photographs of you with known Mafia members... and gangsters spoke of ...*Sinatra.*

What was that all about?

Whatever the truth of it... why cultivate the myth? Did it help make up for Hoboken?

And what about the man inside, **FRANKIE?**... was there anything that could keep you in the moment?... The entire adventure dazzled you... the adoration, the crowds, and the women who loved you... It brought you to an unbroken consciousness. It was never enough. Nothing could ever gratify you. No matter how powerful you became you were still the skinny wop kid from Hoboken.

The nation listened to your voice and knew there was always something in your songs that reflected something back to us... that spoke to us about what it means to be human.

There was something relevant about a man with a velvet voice, who held a significant hold on a nation... a man who brought a special kind of magnificence to our music...

A man whose blue eyes still haunt us

A man who cannot be defined in ordinary words. A man, in the final analysis, who did it his way.

Maria Montessori

"liberator"

Sign in Virgo

Educator

"Free the child's potential, and you will transform him into the world."

MARIA TECLA ARTEMESIA MONTESSORI,

A child is born and her awareness is formed by the five senses. She is equipped with the ability to see, hear, smell, taste and to touch and be touched... and to feel a great range of emotions!

What a miracle that is!

What if, instead of being forced into a preconceived program... she were allowed to have her own experience?...

Her level of activity happens on many levels... What would happen if we allowed her to learn at her own pace?

Imagination!

The door to her universe is opened... her potential is released. How can one share in the excitement of her curiosity, satisfy her hunger for learning, and also honor her yearning for spiritual freedom?

You, **MARIA MONTESSORI,** made a magnificent significant discovery!

It is the teacher who must pay rapt attention to the student, not the other way around!

It takes a very special person to start a revolution like yours, **MARIA.**

At a time when a woman could not walk in the street alone... or do so much as write a check without her husband's consent, you attended the University of Rome and became the first female doctor in Italy. You were a woman who broke tradition and changed the rules... A woman who was interviewed by Queen Victoria and who represented your country at important conferences.

How did it all come to you, **MARIA?** Where did your sense of social responsibility come from? Where your expansive heart... your insight... Your unique ability to observe?...

The power that separated you from all others.

"If I am going up a ladder, and a dog begins to bite my ankles, I can do one of two things – either turn round and kick out of it, or simply go on up the ladder. I prefer to go up the ladder!"

Betrayal

There is so much we don't know about you, **MARIA.**

When did it all start?

Was it when Giuseppe Ferruccio Montesano came into your life?

Handsome, elegant, noble

There was a spiritual continuity between you... a sense of fire and impulse as though you both knew what had brought you together.

It was not a conventional affair. There was a child born out of wedlock... *a son...* Giuseppe promised to love you and never marry anyone else... but he betrayed you a year later with another love.

MARIA, was this the first broken promise that brought you to heartbreak? How could you reconcile your love and your son with the man who betrayed you?

Your strength, **MARIA,** came from the rhythms of the powerful forces inside of you. Your personal universe... expansive and complete... held all the answers in your search for the other side of heartbreak.

A Retreat

MARIA, you searched for a way to handle defeat when it was staring you straight in the eyes.

Did you fold?

No

Your resiliency protected you from the mundane... took you on an odyssey... lifted you away from mediocrity. You went to the Monastery... meditated and looked inside yourself... and emerged a new woman ready to manifest change.

You preserved yourself, moved through your pain... and dared to transform the education system... and change the way children are taught...

...forever

You used your own crisis to become a strong force for your life's work. You said.

"It is the child who makes the man, and no man exists who was not made by the child he once was."

Carlo Tresca

"freedom fighter"

Sun in Pisces

Anarchist

"We believe that the class struggle existing in society is expressed in the economic power of the master on the one side and the growing economic power of the workers on the other side..."

CARLO,

What is a freedom fighter?

The dictionary says, "a freedom fighter is a person who takes part in a resistance movement against an oppressive political or social establishment."

Well, I guess that kind of says is it all----but does it?

You, **CARLO,** were an anarchist, a writer, an agitator and an organizer. You found your passion in the struggle… at a time in America when unions were just being organized and were under siege. You helped organize and win many strikes… you were always fighting for America's working men and women.

What kind of a man gives his life to a movement?

You were charismatic, handsome, and authentic. A man that lived outside of yourself… a fathomless figure living in the contours of your truth. A man who lived the incarnation of his deeds and who was not afraid.

Is it not enough for a man to live his ideals?

You are remembered for your courage as a labor agitator... as an anti-fascist... and yet, so little is known about you.

You were not a man who 'never walked alone'... because you always carried with you a human connection to the world around you. There was always a fight to be won, a struggle to overcome.

Had you discovered something the rest of us have not?

Some secret source to the mysterious regions of humanity? Something to believe in that made you bigger than yourself?

Elizabeth

On May 1, 1912 you met Elizabeth Gurley Flynn. It was May Day. An appropriate day for two freedom fighters to meet. The sun was shining on her dark hair reflecting in her eyes like blue crystals. You were smitten. Elizabeth was one of the most famous political organizers in this early century drama and you inspired each other.

What a partnership that was!

"My life with Carlo was tempestuous, because we were both strong personalities..." Elizabeth wrote. And you wrote to her from prison, **"To the woman who has constantly inspired me, who has spent... her time, her energy, her youth to rescue me from the capitalist bastille."**

Together you lived in the rhythm of your radical ideals, bringing a communion of a man and woman in its most illuminating and positive form. Yet, there is so little you knew about women... and there were infidelities. In May 1925 your relationship ended.

It was a hard and wild time not just for you, **CARLO**, but for all of America...

WWII was at its peak... Franklin Delano Roosevelt announced harsh taxes for the country... and gasoline rationing... Tommy Dorsey's *"There Are such Things"* was the number one song in the country... Americans were watching 'How Green is My Valley' and

'Casablanca' at the movies... Rosie was riveting... Enrico Fermi initiated the first self-sustaining nuclear reaction and across the ocean the British were about to seize Tripoli from Mussolini's army...

January 11, 1943, Monday

You, **CARLO TRESCA**, had enemies. Mussolini put your name on his death list due to your anti-fascist activities in the Italian community... The Mafia had secured you as an enemy for your fight against crime... and the NYPD had you down as a terrorist.

On a cool January evening on the corner of 15th street and Fifth Avenue, a shadow of a man stepped out of the murk holding a revolver. He waited for his target.

You, **CARLO TRESCA**, emerged from your building. It was a dark night and you stood under a streetlight to find your way.

You were shot to death on the streets you fought to keep free.

And so it goes

As I look back over these pages I realize that there is a part of me in every one of these vignettes.

As I look at my life... I see that a door is open... and through it the sun reflects like a mirror.

The open sky is out there... expansive and full of light.

I wonder where all of this will take me... and then I see wildflowers growing outside my door...

Bearing roots that are solidly planted

CIAO

ANNA

BIO

Anna Filameno was born in Little Italy in The Bronx. She has been acting since she was seven years old. During her late teens she travelled with an Agit Prop theater group, which brought her to many parts of the country. She was with The Players Guild in New York City, Karamu Theater in Cleveland, Ohio and the Apple Street Playhouse in New Orleans.

After a long separation from her roots, she began a personal odyssey that brought her to a revelation that she is deeply rooted in her heritage. From this she began writing about her experience and through these vignettes she has been given new insights into the Italian spirit.

Anna was committed to her belief in the human spirit, her imagination and her love for her own emotional liberation. When she is not acting or writing she spent inspiring afternoons with her granddaughter Sofia Rose.

ANNA Passed 1/30/2016

Visit her facebook fan page:
http://goo.gl/hmh9FR

Webpage:
https://annafilameno.net

contact publisher at:
soundartus@gmail.com

Her publisher page is here:
https://store.soundartus.com/adventurous-women/

www.ingramcontent.com/pod-product-compliance
Lightning Source LLC
Chambersburg PA
CBHW040322300426

44112CB00020B/2843